Acknowledgements

Illustrations by Steve Cox
Photographs by Zul Mukhida except for: p. 11t CNT Marketing;
pp. 15, 18 Arcaid; pp. 16, 17t, 17m, 22b, 24b Jenny Matthews;
pp. 17b Harald Lange, 19bl Harald Lange, 23t Dr Charles Henneghien,
Bruce Coleman Limited; p. 19t Jon Davison; pp. 19br Mark Edwards,
27 Jorgen Schytte, Still Pictures; p. 22t Art Directors;
pp. 24t Jacky Chapman, 25br Ulrike Preuss, Format.

The author and publisher would like to thank the staff and pupils of
Balfour Infant School, Brighton.

A CIP catalogue record for this book is available
from the British Library.

ISBN 0-7136-3763-3

First published 1994 by A & C Black (Publishers) Ltd
35 Bedford Row, London WC1R 4JH

Reprinted 1996

Typeset by Rowland Phototypesetting Ltd, Bury St Edmunds, Suffolk
Printed in Belgium by Proost International Book Production

Where people live

Barbara Taylor

Illustrations by Steve Cox

Photographs by Zul Mukhida and Jenny Matthews

Contents

A & C Black · London

A place to live

What is your home like? Is it quiet and peaceful or busy and noisy? Who else lives in your home?

A home is a place where people live. It is a place where we eat and sleep and spend time with our family. There are lots of different types of home. Perhaps you live in a flat, a house or maybe a bungalow?

What do you like most about your home? What spoils it? Is there anything you would change to make it a better place to live?

I'd like my own room.

I'd like a garden.

I'd like somewhere to keep Henry.

Ask your friends what they think is most important about their homes.

You could draw a chart to show what you find out.

It's where I go to sleep.

It's a place to be with my family.

How are homes different from other buildings? Look carefully at the buildings in this street. What is each place used for? Which buildings do people live in?

Where are homes?

Where is your home? Is it in a big city, a town or a small village? Are there other homes nearby, or lots of fields and farms? How far is it to the shops?

See if you can draw a picture of your home area. Close your eyes and think carefully – are there any special features, such as a fire station or village hall?

What do you like and dislike about your home area? Do you have somewhere you like to play? Do your friends live nearby? Do you have to be careful of busy roads?

I like living in the country, but I get a bit lonely.

I like living near to the sports centre, but I wish I had a garden.

If you could live somewhere else, where would you like to live? See if you can build up a picture of your ideal home area using the pictures around the edge of the page to help you. What other things can you think of?

When people are choosing places to build homes, they need to think about things like the shape and cost of the land, where there are roads and railways, how far the homes are from a town or city and where there are places of work. They also need to think about the weather.

Can you work out why these homes are in these places?

(The answers are at the bottom of the page.)

Answers:

1 Holiday homes near to a beach
2 Homes near to a factory
3 Homes near to a railway line and station

10

Sometimes, whole new towns are built. The people building these new towns have to decide where to put schools, shops, workplaces and leisure areas as well as homes.

The planners of Milton Keynes split the town into sections so that the houses, the shops and the workplaces were all in different areas.

Can you find out why your home was built in a particular place? Your library should have pictures and maps of your home area years ago. Has it changed much? Are there more homes today? Can you see a reason for the homes being built, such as a market, a port or a railway line?

Town and country homes

Imagine you are an estate agent who has to sell two homes. One is in the town and the other is in the countryside. Draw a poster telling people about the best points of each home. What sort of things do you need to include?

Here are some ideas, but they are all jumbled up. Can you sort out which go with the town home and which go with the home in the countryside?

roadside parking

big garden

close to shops and school

5 minutes to park

lovely views over farmland

10 minutes to nearest town

If you were going to sell your home, what sort of things would you put in the advert?

These people are all looking for a new place to live.
Which home do you think would be best for them?

Mr and Mrs Brown

Mr and Mrs Cook
Amy and Luke

Mr and Mrs Johnson

- Modern town house
- 2 bedrooms
- 10 minutes to city centre
- Small, paved garden

- Sunny bungalow in quiet country area
- Small garden with patio
- Short walk on flat path to shops and medical centre

- Roomy, detached house with lovely views
- Large garden
- 5 minutes to local school and shops

What are homes made of?

When people build homes they need to think about which materials can be found locally and how much they cost. They also need to think about how strong the materials are and if they are suitable for the weather and climate.

Concrete is very cheap and lasts well in harsh climates.

Bricks are very strong. They last well in all weather.

Wood can be made into all kinds of different shapes, but it has to be painted or varnished to stop it going rotten.

Earth walls are good in hot weather but they wash away in the rain.

Homes are built from lots of different materials. What is your home made of? Are the walls made of different materials from the roof? What about the window-frames and the doors? Are they made of wood, metal or plastic?

How many different materials have been used to build these homes?

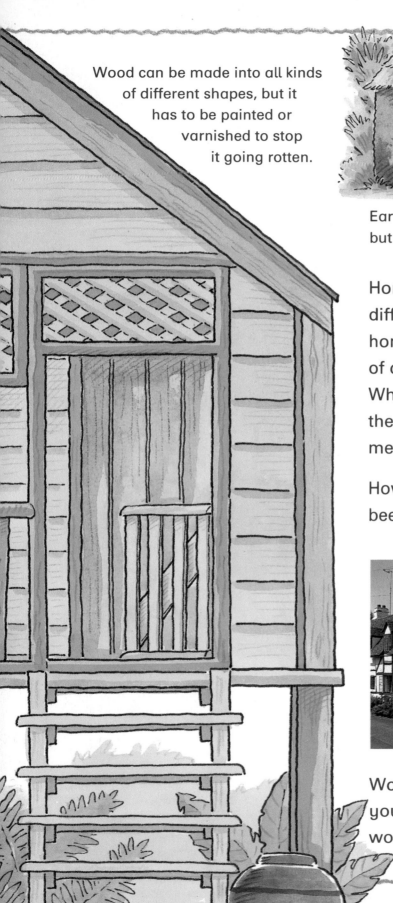

Would you like to design and build your own home? Which materials would you use?

Look carefully at these photographs of homes in other parts of the world. How many different materials can you see? What do you think the weather is like in each place? Find each of the countries on a map of the world.

This home in Ethiopia is made out of wood. It has a thatched roof.

This home in Namibia is made from corrugated iron.

This home in Kosovo, in former Yugoslavia, is made from concrete and bricks. The windows have wooden shutters.

This home in Haiti is made from palm leaves.

Some people live in homes which can be moved from place to place. The type of home they live in often depends on the transport they have.

People who travel around on an animal, such as a horse or camel, or on foot, need to have homes which are easy to pack up, and small and light enough to carry around.

Other people adapt their homes to suit a particular type of transport.

This woman is part of a family of travellers who live in caravans.

This man has turned his canal boat into a home.

These Bedouin people travel around the Sahara Desert in Morocco. They live in tents made out of woollen blankets.

What do homes look like?

The style of the homes in your area will tell you a lot about the history of the place and the people that have lived there. You could go on a home-spotting walk in your local area. How many different styles of home can you find? Do any of them have any special features? Can you find out when they were built? Were any of the homes built for a special reason?

These tenement houses were built in 1892. Each building was divided into flats to house a number of separate families.

This Edwardian home was built in the early 1900's.

This semi-detached home was built in the 1930's.

Some people want to change their homes to make them stand out from the rest. Others like their homes to look like all the rest.

The owner of this home in Oxford has made it look very different from the others in his street.

The climate of an area can also affect the way a home is built. Look carefully at these two pictures. The home on the left has been built in a place where the weather is cold. The home on the right has been built in a place where the weather is hot. What differences can you see?

This home in Iceland is painted black to absorb the heat of the Sun. The grass roof and built-up walls help to keep the heat in.

This home in Sri Lanka is painted white to reflect the heat of the Sun. Its large overhanging roof provides plenty of shade.

A new place to live

Have you ever moved home? What did it feel like? Moving home is exciting because you can make new friends and go to see new places. But moving home is a bit scary, too, because so many things change and you might miss your old friends. It takes time to get used to a new place.

What sort of things would you need to think about if you were going to move home? Perhaps you'd want to find out about your new school or if there were any other children living nearby. Here are some other ideas.

Is there somewhere to play?

Where's everything going to go?

Can I help decorate my room?

post office

park

school

swimming pool

library

Anna and her mother have just moved to Busytown. This is a map of Busytown with Anna's home marked by a red cross. Can you help Anna and her mother find the way to her new school, the park, the library, the post office and the swimming pool?

You need to tell Anna and her mother when to turn left or right and when to go straight on. Are there any short cuts they can take if they are walking instead of going by car?

Anna wrote this letter to her friend soon after she moved home.

Pretend you have moved to a new home. What sort of letter would you write to your best friend?

Dear Sam,
The new house is full of boxes and I can't find my panda. I'm going to my new school next week and I'm a bit scared.
Mum says you can come and stay. Please write to me soon.
Lots of love Anna x x x

Some people choose to move home. They may need a bigger or a smaller home or want to live nearer to their friends and relations. Some people move just because they feel like a change.

But sometimes, people have to move home. They may get a job in another part of the country or become ill and need to live nearer to their relatives.

Moving home.

There are also people, called refugees, who have been forced to leave their homes. Their homes may have been destroyed in a natural disaster, such as an earthquake or a flood, or they may have left their homes because of the threat of war or famine.

Although refugees have to leave their homes, they may find new homes in another country or be able to go back to their old homes one day.

This family is living in a refugee camp on the West Bank of the river Jordan.

Some people are always on the move, taking their homes with them. They may do this because they like the freedom or because they need to find work or food for their animals.

People who are always on the move can only take a few things with them on their journeys.

These people are part of a tribe travelling near Biskra, in Algeria. They can fit themselves and all their belongings on to their camel.

Imagine you had to pack everything you need at home into a rucksack. Which things would you choose?

Nowhere to live

There are many reasons why people are homeless. People who can't find work or who lose their job are often unable to find enough money to pay for their home. Some young people become homeless because they want to leave home, but have nowhere else to live.

A homeless man asleep on the street in Los Angeles, USA.

Homeless people living on the streets in Rio de Janeiro, Brazil.

Imagine what it would be like to be homeless. Which of these home comforts would you miss most?

When people do not have a home, it's hard for them to get a job. It is also difficult for homeless people to keep clean and warm, so they are often ill. In many countries there is little help for people who fall on hard times and lose their homes.

Charities run hostels for the homeless to provide food and shelter, but often there are not enough places to go round.

This homeless man is selling The Big Issue, a magazine set up to help the homeless.

Living on planet Earth

How do homes change the environment?
This picture shows what goes into
a home and what comes out.

what goes in ▽
1 electricity   2 gas
3 water   4 food
5 fresh air

what comes out △
1 rubbish   2 dirty water
3 sewage   4 heat
5 pollution

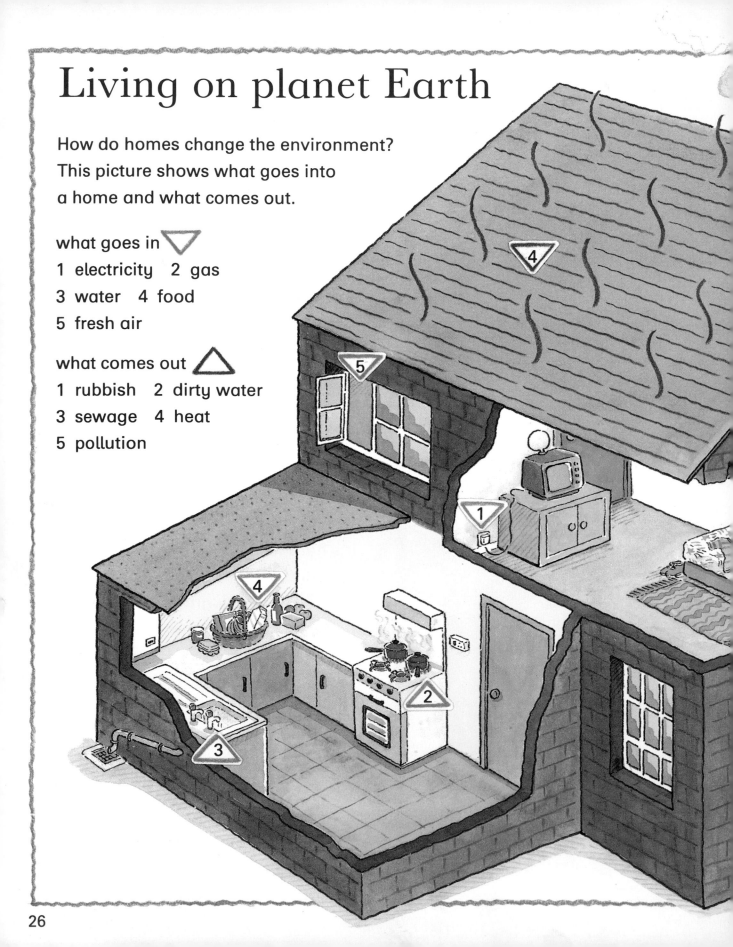

The dirty things coming out of our homes can be harmful to the environment. Can you think of anything we can do to help?

Homes use up huge amounts of energy. Nowadays, it is possible to design homes, like the one in the photograph, so that they don't waste energy.

A solar heated home in India.

But planet Earth is getting very crowded. In the future, people may have to live underground or in cities that float on the sea. We may even have to move out to other planets. Would you like to live on a planet such as Mars?

Index

For parents and teachers
More about the ideas in this book

Pages 6/7 These pages look at the purpose of a home and the children's feelings about it, rather than details of physical features and buildings. Talking about imaginary homes may avoid upsetting those children for whom home is not a happy place.

Pages 8/11 The location of homes is affected by the landscape, the weather, the wealth of the people and the position of existing towns and cities. Children can compare their home area with another contrasting area. Links with history topics can be made by looking at old maps, postcards or books of places in the past.

Pages 12/13 Country homes are usually quieter than town homes, with bigger gardens and less polluted air. They are, however, often a long way from workplaces and have less choice of shopping and entertainment facilities.

Pages 14/19 Building materials vary depending on the landscape, the climate and the availability and cost of the materials (one third of all the people in the world live in earth houses). Links with history topics can be made by looking at the physical appearance of homes. The permanent or temporary nature of homes is also introduced here.

Pages 20/23 Use the children's own experiences of moving home to lead on to the idea of people who never settle in one place. Refugee issues are complex and can only be touched on at this level.

Pages 24/25 Homelessness occurs all over the world. Encourage the children to explore the reasons for homelessness, both practical and social, and the ways different countries may try to help homeless people.

Pages 26/27 Wherever people live, they inevitably use up energy and pollute the environment. Encourage the children to find out what other countries are doing to make homes 'greener'. Building new homes also reduces the amount of space left for wildlife.

Things to do

Going places provides starting points for all kinds of cross-curricular work based on geography and the environment, both on a local and a global scale. **Where people live** explores the use of buildings for homes, and looks at how homes are influenced by landscape, weather, wealth, availability and cost of materials, environmental and urban issues. Here are some ideas for follow-up activities to extend the ideas further.

1 To look more closely at a variety of homes in their local area, children could make drawings or models of the homes in their street. How many different styles of homes are there? What special features do the different homes have? What does the outward appearance of a home tell you about the people who live inside?

2 Make a collection of pictures to illustrate the different building styles around the world, such as Dutch gables, North American clapperboard homes, Tudor beams, Islamic domes, Roman or Greek arches, West Indian bungalows, castles, high-rise flats in Nairobi or Rio, elaborate earth homes in Yemen, houses on stilts in Indonesia. What influences the different building styles?

3 Children could draw a map of a room in their home or a map of their ideal bedroom. They could also draw a map of the route to a friend's home.

4 Make a collection of advertisements for homes from estate agents. Separate the pictures of the homes from their details. Children could make up their own home details by looking at the pictures or read the details and draw their own picture of the home. Alternatively, children could match up the pictures with their correct descriptions.

5 Drama activities could be developed from topics such as moving home, the life of a nomad or the journeys of a traveller's home.

Encourage the children to think about how they'd feel if their home was always on the move, or if they had to leave all their friends behind and start at a new school, perhaps in another country.

6 To build on the theme of imaginary homes, children could pretend to be town planners and design a new village. What sort of homes do people want? What is the weather like? What sort of local building materials are available? How many homes are needed? What sort of special features would be necessary in a home for a disabled person? The village could be on another planet to allow for more imaginative work.

7 Experiment with the properties of different building materials, both natural and artificial. Properties such as strength, flexibility, texture and weight are important in building homes. The children could try making mud bricks or walls of woven straw. How do environmental problems, such as acid rain, affect building materials? Which materials are good insulators and keep buildings warm? How are building materials joined together? Investigate the different shapes used in building homes, such as tubes, frames, domes and arches.

8 Find out about the different types of homes built by animals. Many animals build temporary or permanent homes to shelter from the weather, to hide from predators or to protect their young. Chimpanzees build nests to sleep in, rabbits and prairie dogs dig burrows, wasps build nests of paper and birds build complex nests of twigs, grass, moss and feathers. Animals such as spiders and bees produce their own building materials (silk and wax) inside their bodies.

9 Find out about the technology of 'green' homes, such as insulation in walls and roofs, energy-saving devices, including those in traditional homes such as Adobi dwellings and the use of solar or wind power.